THE BIG LITTLE BOOK OF
JEWISH WIT & WISDOM

THE BIG LITTLE BOOK OF

JEWISH

WIT & WISDOM

EDITED BY SALLY BERK

ILLUSTRATIONS BY MARIA CARLUCCIO

BD&L

Library of Congress Cataloging-in-Publication Data

The big little book of Jewish wit and wisdom / edited by Sally Ann Berk.
p.   cm.
Includes bibliographical references.
ISBN 1-57912-146-2 (hc)
Jewish wit and humor. 2. Jews—Social life and customs—Literary collections. I.
Berk, Sally Ann.

PN6231.J5 B47 2000
808.88'2'089924--dc21

00-030356

Book design: 27.12 design ltd. (New York)

Printed in Hong Kong

Black Dog & Leventhal Publishers, Inc.
151 West 19th Street
New York, New York 10011

Distributed by
Workman Publishing Company
708 Broadway
New York, New York 10003

h g f e d c b a

DEDICATION

This book is dedicated to my family. To my Aunt Florence Lippman, who spent a lot of time, and had a lot of fun, digging up favorite family expressions and stories; to my great-aunt Ruth Preis, who remembered many, many very expressive curses and tales and relayed them to me with delight; to my father, Stanley Berk, who told me a lot of bad jokes, and some good ones, and who helped his sister Florence remember; and to my mother Marjorie Berk, a woman of valor and chutzpah. She is my yogi and my inspiration. And of course, to my husband James Wakeman, a real mensch, and my beautiful son Max Berk-Wakeman.

This book is also dedicated to the memory of my beloved grandparents, Sol and Celia Berkovitz and Morris and Leona Soltz, and my great-grandparents Morris and Frances Bloom, and Joseph and Fanny Soltz. Although Maimonides said that one should not mourn for longer than a month, not a day goes by that I don't hear one of my grandparents whispering in my ear, offering advice and love. I miss them still.

—*Sally Ann Berk*

CONTENTS

You can always wash your hands.

—*Sally Sternberg*

Iron the sleeves first.

—*Leona Soltz*

THE LIFE CYCLE

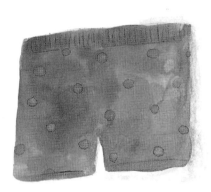

I don't believe in an afterlife, although
I am bringing a change of underwear.

—*Woody Allen*

What is painful to one generation
is insight for the next.

—*Eli N. Evans*

I will never be an old man. To me, old
age is always fifteen years older than I am.

—*Bernard Baruch*

When I was a boy, the Dead Sea was just sick.

—*George Burns*

Becky at eighty: I'm obsessed
with the hereafter.
Every time I walk into a room,
I have to ask myself,
"What am I here after?"

—*David Shore*

It is a sobering thought,
that when Mozart was my age
he had been dead for two years.

—*Tom Lehrer*

I think your whole life shows in your
face and you should be proud of that.

—*Lauren Bacall*

For dying, you always have time.

The only truly dead
are those who have been forgotten.

After thirty,
a body has a mind of its own.

—*Bette Midler*

One does not get better, but different
and older and that is always a pleasure.

—*Gertrude Stein*

From birth to age eighteen,
a girl needs good parents,
from eighteen to thirty-five
she needs good looks,
from thirty-five to fifty-five
she needs a good personality,
and from fifty-five on she needs good
cash. I'm saving my money.

—*Sophie Tucker*

An eighty-year-old man walks into a
confessional and says,
"Forgive me Father, for I have sinned.
I just spent the entire night having sex
with two eighteen-year-old girls."
The priest asks,
"How long since your last confession,
my son?"
The old man laughs and says,
"Confession?
I've never been to confession.
I'm Jewish."
The priest asks,
"Why are you telling me this?"
The old man replies,
"Telling YOU?
I'm telling EVERYBODY!"

I don't want to achieve immortality through my work. I want to achieve it through not dying.

—*Woody Allen*

Gray hair is a crown of glory. It is attained by a life of righteousness.

—*Proverbs*

The virtue of angels is that they cannot deteriorate; their flaw is that they cannot improve. Humanity's flaw is that we can deteriorate; but our virtue is that we can improve.

For the ignorant, old age is winter; for the learned, it is the harvest.

—*Hasidic saying*

There is a big controversy these days
concerning when life begins.
In Jewish tradition the fetus is not considered a viable human being until after
graduation from medical school.

For old age is not honored
for length of time, nor measured by
number of years;
but understanding is gray hair for men,
and a blameless life is ripe old age.

—*Solomon*

You have to learn to do everything,
even to die.

—*Gertrude Stein*

The turning point in the process of
growing up is when you discover the
core strength within you that survives
all hurt.

—*Max Lerner*

You're never too old to become younger.

—*Mae West*

The whole business of marshaling one's energies becomes more and more important as one grows older.

—*Hume Cronyn*

The great secret that all old people share is that you really haven't changed in seventy or eighty years. Your body changes, but you don't change at all. And that, of course, causes great confusion.

—*Doris Lessing*

23

Morty is on his deathbed.
He raises his head slowly, and calls for
his wife. "Gittel, are you there?"
"Yes, Morty, I'm here." A moment
later Morty says, "Danny, are you
there?" His son, Danny assures him
he's by his side. "Davey," says the ailing
Morty, "Are you there?" "I'm here,
Papa," said his other son Davey, taking
his hand. With all the strength he can
muster, Morty raises himself up
on his elbows and yells, "Then who the
hell is minding the store?"

There's a thing that keeps surprising you about stormy old friends after they die—their silence. For a while an echo stays in your ear. You hear a laugh, a knowing phrase or two, a certain quality of enunciation. Then, nothing. Another death takes place—voices.

—*Ben Hecht*

Middle Age: When pulling an all nighter means not having to get up to go to the bathroom.

—*Michael Feldman*

Old age and sickness bring out the essential characteristics of a man.

—*Felix Frankfurter*

Every death leaves a scar, and every time a child laughs it starts healing.

—*Eli Weisel*

Age is strictly a case of mind over matter.
If you don't mind, it doesn't matter.

—*Jack Benny*

Every man knows he must die, but no
one believes it.

When a righteous man dies, he dies only
for his generation. It is like a man who loses
a pearl. Wherever it may be, it continues to
be a pearl. It is lost only to its owner.

—*The Talmud*

An elderly man goes to the doctor complaining of aches and pains all over his body. After a thorough examination, the doctor gives him a clean bill of health. "Hymie, you're in fine shape for an eighty year old. After all, I'm not a magician—I can't make you any younger," says the doctor. "Who asked you to make me younger? Just make sure I get older!"

Learning in old age is like writing on sand; learning in youth is like engraving on stone.

—*Solomon Ibn Gabirol*

You shall plan your work, choose your tools, and number your offspring so that one generation after your death, the earth is as whole, healthy, and holy as it was one generation before you were born.

—*Rabbi Arthur Waksow*

In his will, my grandfather stipulated:
Take care of your grandmother.
Preserve your Yiddishkeit. I don't want
any monuments. If people read my
books, that will be my best monument.
Read one of my stories aloud in
whatever language is convenient.

—*Bel Kaufman, granddaughter of Sholom Aleichem*

Youth is the gift of nature,
but age is work of art.

—*Garson Kanin*

It is always self-defeating to pretend to the style of a generation younger than your own; it simply erases your experience in history.

—*Renata Adler*

In the hour of a person's departure, neither silver nor gold nor precious stones nor pearls accompany them, but only Torah and good works.

—*Ethics of the Fathers*

A baby enters the world with hands clenched as if to say, "The world is mine: I shall grab it." A man leaves with his hands open, as if to say, "I can take nothing with me."

–Midrash

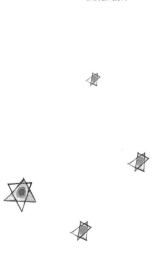

"You're in great shape," says the doctor.
"You're going to live to be seventy."
"But I am seventy," the patient replies.
"Nu," says the doctor, "did I lie?"

THE GETTING OF WISDOM

Behind every argument
is someone's ignorance.

—*Louis Brandeis*

Words are like bodies,
and meanings like souls.

—*Ibn Ezra*

The simple believes everything.

—*Proverbs*

A man should never cast his reason
behind him, for the eyes are set in
front, not in back.

—*Moses Maimonides*

Desperation is sometimes as powerful
an inspirer as genius.

—*Benjamin Disraeli*

There are perhaps no days of our
childhood we lived so fully as those we
spent with a favorite book.

—*Marcel Proust*

Everybody gets so much information
all day long that they lose
their common sense.

—*Gertrude Stein*

Somewhere, something incredible is
waiting to be known.

—*Carl Sagan*

Nobody could get involved with a half a million youngsters and be the same afterward as he was before.

—*Max Yasgur*

It makes no difference whether you study in the holy language, or in Arabic or Aramaic; it matters only whether it is done with understanding.

—*Moses Maimonides*

The wise man hears one word and understands two.

Education is learning what you didn't even know you didn't know.

—*Daniel J. Boorstin*

Do not say, "When I have leisure I shall study," perhaps you will never have leisure.

—*Rabbi Hillel*

For wisdom is better than rubies, and all things desirable are not to be compared unto her.

—*Proverbs*

Give to a wise man, and he will be yet wiser; teach a righteous man, and he will increase in learning.

—*Proverbs*

It's so simple to be wise. Just think of something stupid to say and say the opposite.

—*Sam Levenson*

He that does not add to his store of knowledge decreases it.

—*Rabbi Hillel*

If there be no understanding, there is no knowledge, if there be no knowledge, there is no understanding.

—*Rabbi Elazar ben Azariah*

I was born not knowing and have only had a little time to change that here and there.

—*Richard Feynman*

Lulu and her grandfather are walking in the park. Lulu asks him, "Pop-pop, why do trees have leaves?" Pop-pop says, "What am I, a botanist? How should I know?" A little while later, they see some birds eating worms. "Pop-pop," Lulu asks, "why do birds eat worms?" "What am I, the Birdman of Alcatraz?" Soon, they see a woman walking her dog. "Pop-pop, why is that dog walking sideways?" "If I know why that dog walks sideways, I'd be a veterinarian," replies Pop-pop. In a bit, Lulu asks "Pop-pop, can I ask you another question?" "Of course," says Pop-pop, "How else are you going to learn anything?"

Books are the carriers of civilization.
Without books, history is silent,
literature dumb, science crippled.

—*Barbara Tuchman*

One who walks with the wise grows wise,
but a companion of fools suffers harm.

—*Proverbs*

It is a duty to honor every scholar,
even if he's not one's teacher.

—*Moses Maimonides*

In seeking wisdom
the first step is silence;
the second, listening;
the third, remembering;
the fourth, practicing;
the fifth, teaching others.

—*Solomon Ibn Gabirol*

The only rational way of educating is to
be an example of what to avoid,
if one can't be the other sort.

—*Albert Einstein*

People were given two ears
and one tongue
so that they may listen
more than speak.

Be happy. It is a way of being wise.

—*Colette*

We are at the very beginning of time for the human race. It is not unreasonable that we grapple with problems. But there are tens of thousands of years in the future. Our responsibility is to do what we can, learn what we can, improve the solutions, and pass them on.

—*Richard P. Feynman*

Wonder, rather than doubt, is the root of knowledge.

—*Abraham Joshua Heschel*

A great deal of intelligence can be invested in ignorance when the need for illusion is deep.

—*Saul Bellow*

No one has yet realized the wealth of sympathy, the kindness and generosity hidden in the soul of a child.
The effort of every true education should be to unlock that treasure.

—*Emma Goldman*

A bookstore is one of the only pieces of
evidence we have that people
are still thinking.

—*Jerry Seinfeld*

Good questions out rank easy answers.

—*Paul A. Samuelson*

We make our world significant by the courage of our questions, and by the depth of our answers.

—*Carl Sagan*

An expert is a man who has made all the mistakes that can be made, in a very narrow field.

—*Niels Bohr*

During my eighty-seven years
I have witnessed a whole succession
of technological revolutions. But none
of them has done away with the need for
character in the individual or the ability
to think.

—*Bernard M. Baruch*

That is what learning is.
You suddenly understand something
you've understood all your life,
but in a new way.

—*Doris Lessing*

A wise man's question
contains half the answer.

—*Solomon Ibn Gabirol*

The lessons of youth are not easily forgotten.

—*The Talmud*

To some questions there is no answer,
and to other questions there are too
many answers.

—*Sholem Asch*

Trust yourself,
you know more than you think you do.

—*Benjamin Spock, M.D.*

I am enough of an artist
to draw freely upon my imagination.
Imagination is more important than
knowledge. Knowledge is limited.
Imagination encircles the world.

—*Albert Einstein*

The opposite of a correct statement
is a false statement. The opposite of a
profound truth may well be another
profound truth.

—*Niels Bohr*

Consistency requires you to be
as ignorant today as you were a year ago.

—*Bernard Berenson*

The luck of the fool is that he doesn't know that he doesn't know.

Tombstones need not be erected on the graves of the righteous.
Their teachings are their monuments.

—*The Talmud*

God loves truthfulness
above piety and learning.

Where all men think alike, no one
thinks very much.

—*Walter Lippmann*

Who is ignorant?
He who does not educate his children.

—*The Talmud*

The highest form of wisdom
is kindness.

—*The Talmud*

RELIGION, GOD
& SPIRITUALITY

An atheist may be simply one whose faith and love are concentrated on the impersonal aspects of God.

—*Simone Weil*

To know what is impenetrable to us really exists, manifesting itself as the highest wisdom and the most radiant beauty . . . this knowledge, this feeling is at the center of true religiousness.

—*Albert Einstein*

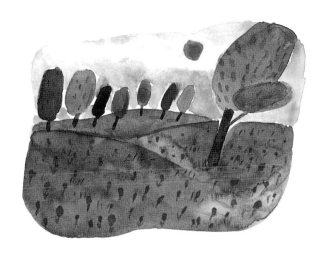

Every blade of grass has its angel that
bends over it and whispers, grow, grow.

—*The Talmud*

There is no such thing as inner peace.
There is only nervousness or death.
Any attempt to prove otherwise
constitutes unacceptable behavior.

—*Fran Lebowitz*

It is the experience of living that is
important, not searching for meaning.
We bring meaning
by how we love the world.

—*Bernie S. Siegal*

The opposite of love is not hate,
it's indifference.
The opposite of art is not ugliness,
it's indifference.
The opposite of faith is not heresy,
it's indifference.
And the opposite of life is not death,
it's indifference.

—*Elie Wiesel*

Duty cannot exist without faith.

—*Benjamin Disraeli*

Vision looks inwards and
becomes duty. Vision looks outwards
and becomes aspiration. Vision looks
upwards and becomes faith.

—*Stephen Wise*

The world is new to us every
morning—and every man should believe
he is reborn each day.

—*Baal Shem Tov*

Religion is comparable to a childhood neurosis.

—*Sigmund Freud*

There are only two ways to live your life. One is as though nothing is a miracle. The other is as though everything is a miracle.

—*Albert Einstein*

Not only is there no God, but try getting a plumber on weekends.

—*Woody Allen*

I am a creature of God and my neighbor is also a creature of God. I work in the city and he works in the country. I rise early for my work and he rises early for his work. Just as he cannot excel in my work, I cannot excel in his work. Will you say that I do great things and he does small things? We have learned that it does not matter whether a person does much or little, as long as he directs his heart to heaven.

—*The Talmud*

Doubt is part of all religion.
All the religious thinkers were doubters.

—*Isaac Bashevis Singer*

Science without **religion** is lame.
Religion without science is blind.

—*Albert Einstein*

Ruler of the Universe! I admit that I
have sinned a great deal against you,
but have You granted me only honey?
I have forgiven You for all of the
suffering, the hardship and the torment,
but You must also forgive me.

—*Rabbi Yosef of Brod*

Whoever does not see God in every
place does not see God in any place.

—*Rabbi Menachem Mendel of Kotzk*

Even after one has achieved the spirituality of an angel, one must still abide by the commandments like a simple Jew.

—*Baal Shem Tov*

Righteous people are not perfect beings who never make mistakes, who never experience burnout. Rather, righteous people are those who despite everything, despite falling, despite burnout, stand up, start all over again, and continue to express their loyalty to our Heavenly Father.

—*Esther Jungreis*

God will forgive me; it is his trade.

—*Heinrich Heine*

I cannot conceive of a God
who rewards and punishes
his creatures, or has a will of the kind
that we experience in ourselves.

—*Albert Einstein*

People are accustomed to
look at the Heavens and wonder
what happens there,
it would be better if they would look
within themselves,
to see what happens there.

—*Rabbi Menachem Mendel of Kotsk*

Can He be God if He can only be
worshipped in one way?

—*The Seer of Lublin (Rabbi Yitzhak Yaacov)*

If triangles had a God,
He'd have three sides.

—*Yiddish saying*

Creationists make it sound as though a
'theory' is something you dreamt up
after being drunk all night.

—*Isaac Asimov*

The fairest thing we can experience
is the mysterious. It is the fundamental
emotion which stands at the cradle
of true art and true science.

—*Albert Einstein*

All the 613 commandments
are included in the
Ten Commandments.

—*Rashi*

God exists since mathematics is
consistent, and the Devil exists since we
cannot prove it.

—*André Weil*

Forget not the day of the Sabbath,
Its mention is like a pleasant offering.
During it the dove found resting place,
And there the weary may relax.

—*Yehuda ha-Levi*

If God wills, even a broomstick can shoot.

Everything is foreseen,
but man is given free will.

—Ethics of the Fathers

Music can name the unnamable and
communicate the unknowable.

—Leonard Bernstein

Man plans, and God laughs.

The best remedy for those who are afraid, lonely, or unhappy is to go outside, somewhere where they can be quite alone with the heavens, nature, and G-d. Because only then does one feel that all is as it should be and that G-d wishes to see people happy, amidst the simple beauty of nature. As long as this exists, and it certainly always will, I know that then there will always be comfort for every sorrow.

—*Anne Frank*

Just to be is a blessing.
Just to live is holy.

—*Abraham Heschel*

The Sabbath day is for being with
ourselves, a day of armistice in the
economic struggle with our fellow man
and the forces of nature.

—*Abraham Joshua Heschel*

Some people talk to themselves.
Some people sing to themselves.
Is one group better than the other?
Did not God create all people equal?
Yes God created all people equal.
Only to some he gave the ability to make
up their own words.

—*Fran Lebowitz*

Religion should be the rule of life, not
a casual incident.

—*Benjamin Disraeli*

With faith, there are no questions;
without faith there are no answers.

—*The Chofetz Chaim*

Far more than Israel has kept the
Sabbath, it is the Sabbath
that has kept Israel.

—*Achad Ha'Am*

When the solution is simple,
God is answering.

—*Albert Einstein*

MOTHERS

A mother understands
what a child does not say.

"Mrs. Ginsberg," says the psychiatrist,
"there's nothing physically wrong with
your little boy. But I have to tell you,
he has an Oedipus complex."
"Oedipus-shmedipus! As long as he
loves his mother!"

A child who has all his teeth still needs
his mother to sing him to sleep.

—*Mordkhe Gebirtig*

God could not be everywhere so She
created mothers.

There is no bad mother and no good death.

A Freudian slip is when you say one thing but mean your mother.

The whole motivation for any performer is "Look at me, Ma."

—*Lenny Bruce*

Mothers remember a child's first words, and quote them in terms usually reserved for Byron. Only a mother remembers her children's landmarks as her own.

—*Letty Cottin Pogrebin*

My mother. What can I say about such a wonderful, loving, and caring woman? She kept busy all day cleaning, cooking, and killing . . . mainly chickens. On Friday nights anything with feathers was a goner. That woman plucked till dawn.

—*Mel Brooks*

"What kind of a son is it that doesn't call his mother all week to ask how she feels?" "OK, Mama, how do you feel?" "Don't ask!"

When we were smoking, my mother use to come and say to me, "if you smoke it will stunt your growth." And we used to laugh, "What does she know?" Then, when they hired that midget for Philip Morris, until the day my mother died, she said, "See what happens when you smoke cigarettes? You end up a midget with a cookie on your head."

—*Alan King*

A mother gives her son two sweaters.
To show her how much he likes them,
the next time he sees her he wears one of
them. "What's the matter?" she asks,
"You didn't like the other one?"

The first Jewish President is elected. He calls his Mother and says, "Mama, I've won the election. You've got to come to the inauguration." "I don't know, what would I wear?" "Don't worry, I'll send you a dressmaker." "But I only eat kosher food." "Mama, I am going to be the president. I can get you kosher food." "But how will I get there?" "I'll send a limo. Just come, mama." "OK, OK, if it makes you happy." The great day comes and Mama is seated between the Supreme Court Justices and the future Cabinet members. She nudges the gentleman on her right. "You see that boy, the one giving the speech? His brother's a doctor!"

Did you hear about the homeless man
who walked up to the Jewish mother on
the street and said,
"Lady, I haven't eaten in three days."
"Force yourself," she replied.

The toughest room I ever played was my
mother's kitchen.

—*Richard Belzer*

A young Jewish man calls his mother and says, "Mama, I'm bringing home a wonderful woman that I want to marry. She is a Native American and her name is — 'Shooting Star.'" "How nice," says his mother. "I have an Indian name too—it is 'Sitting Bull.'" You have to call me that from now on." "How nice," says his mother. "I have an Indian name now too, dear. Just call me "Sitting Shiva."

If you want to understand any woman you must first ask about her mother and then listen carefully. Stories about food show a strong connection. Wistful silences demonstrate unfinished business. The more a daughter knows the details of her mother's life—without flinching or whining—the stronger the daughter.

—*Anita Diamant*

When a man's with his friends he makes wife jokes. When he's with his wife he makes mother jokes. And when he's with his mother . . . he lets her make the jokes.

—*Harvey Fierstein*

A Jewish man calls his mother in Florida. He says, "How are you, Mama?" She answers, "Not too good. I've been very weak." The son asks, "Why are you so weak?" "Because I haven't eaten in thirty-eight days." The son asks, "How come you haven't eaten in thirty-eight days?" She said, "Because I didn't want my mouth should be filled with food when you call."

Q: How many Jewish Mothers does it take to change a lightbulb?

A: It's all right . . . I'll sit in the dark.

What's a Jewish sweater?
It is the woolen garment worn by a
child when his mother is cold.

WORKING

Success has made failures of many men.

—*Cindy Adams*

My first piece of advice is to "be lucky."
That's not always easy, but one of the
tricks is to recognize opportunity when
it knocks.

—*Edgar M. Bronfman*

Property is a nuisance.

—*Paul Erdös*

Bankruptcy is a legal proceeding in which you put your money in your pants pocket and give your coat to your creditors.

—*Joey Adams*

As a cousin of mine once said about money, money is always there but the pockets change; it is not in the same pockets after a change, and that is all there is to say about money.

—*Gertrude Stein*

It takes twenty years to become an
overnight success.

—*Eddie Cantor*

Some men are born mediocre, some
men achieve mediocrity, and some men
have mediocrity thrust upon them.

—*Joseph Heller*

Never invest your money in anything
that eats or needs repairing.

—*Billy Rose*

I've got to keep breathing. It'll be my
worst business mistake if I don't.

—*Sir Nathan Rothschild*

No labor, however humble,
is dishonoring.

—*The Talmud*

He who hesitates is last.

—*Mae West*

No man is impatient with his creditors.

—*The Talmud*

When I was born, I owed twelve dollars.

—*George S. Kaufman*

Money is applause.

—*Jacqueline Susann*

I've got all the money I'll ever need
if I die by four o'clock .

—*Henny Youngman*

If you want to know what God thinks
of money, just look at the people
he gave it to.

—*Dorothy Parker*

Be on your guard with the ruling
power, for they bring no one near to
them except for their own interests;
seeming to be friends such time as it is
to their own advantage, they stand not
with a man in the hour of need.

—*Ethics of the Fathers*

Happy is the man who finds wisdom,
the man who gets understanding.
For the gaining of it is better than the
gaining of silver, The profit of it better
than fine gold.

—*Proverbs*

Wealth gained dishonestly dwindles
away, but he who gathers by hand
makes it grow.

—*Proverbs*

Charge nothing
and you'll get a lot of customers.

The powerful person is one who is
master over himself.

—*Ethics of the Fathers*

One who saves his money is wealthier
than one who earns it.

—*Yiddish saying*

A carpenter without tools
is not a carpenter.

—*Midrash*

I am absolutely convinced that no
wealth in the world can help humanity
forward, even in the hand of the most
devoted worker. The example of great
and pure characters is the only thing
that can produce fine ideas and noble
deeds. Money only appeals to selfishness
and always tempts its owner irresistibly
to abuse it.

—*Albert Einstein*

Advertising is 85% confusion
and 15% commission.

—*Fred Allen*

Money is better than poverty,
if only for financial reasons.

—*Woody Allen*

The secret of success
is constancy to purpose.

—*Benjamin Disraeli*

There's nothing so useless
as doing efficiently that which should
not be done at all.

—*Peter F. Drucker*

It has become appallingly obvious
that our technology has
exceeded our humanity.

—*Albert Einstein*

The secret of success is sincerity.
Once you can fake that you've got it made.

—Daniel Schorr

If we could sell our experience for what
they cost us, we'd all be millionaires.

—Abigail Van Buren

There's no such thing as a free lunch.

—Milton Friedman

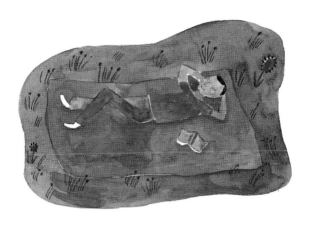

Labor is a craft,
but perfect rest is an art.

—*Abraham Joshua Heschel*

The best way to have a good idea is to have lots of ideas.

—*Linus Pauling*

The most important thing in communication is to hear what isn't being said.

—*Peter F. Drucker*

A decision will be made before it's too late or soon thereafter.

—*Michael Eisner*

A speculator is one who thinks and plans for a future event—and acts before it occurs.

—*Bernard Baruch*

The sad truth is that excellence makes people nervous.

—*Shana Alexander*

"My son," says Mrs. Levy, "is a physicist." "My son," says Mrs. Greenberg, "is Chief of Surgery at Cedars Sinai." "My son," says Mrs. Goldblatt, "is Senior Partner at his law firm and president of the bar association." "My son," says Mrs. Miller, "is a rabbi." "A rabbi? What kind of career is that for a Jewish boy?"

Money is only a tool. It will take you wherever you wish, but it will not replace you as the driver.

—*Ayn Rand*

I always say, keep a diary and some day it'll keep you.

—*Mae West*

Everyone should carefully observe which way his heart draws him, and then choose that way with all his strength.

Happiness does not come from doing easy work but from the afterglow of satisfaction that comes after the achievement of a difficult task that demanded our best.

—*Theodore I. Rubin*

A musician must make music, an artist must paint, a poet must write, if he is to be ultimately at peace with himself. What one can be, one must be.

—*Abraham Maslow*

Whatever you want to do, do it now. There are only so many tomorrows.

—*Michael Landon*

You cannot be anything if you want to be everything.

—*Solomon Schechter*

Don't open a shop unless you know how to smile.

The middle of a rainstorm is not the time to start fixing the hole in the roof.

He was a self-made man who owed his lack of success to nobody.

—*Joseph Heller*

Some people think they are worth a lot
of money just because they have it.

—*Fanny Hurst*

A doctor who charges nothing
is worth nothing.

I have been poor and I have been rich.
Believe me, rich is better.

—*Sophie Tucker*

I do want to get rich, but I never want to do what there is to do to get rich.

—*Gertrude Stein*

Whatever you have to your discredit, be the first to tell it.

Man ought to remember his difficult days in his days of prosperity. He will thereby be inclined to thank God repeatedly and to live a humble life.

—*Moses Maimonides*

MEN & WOMEN

Women complain about premenstrual syndrome, but I think of it as the only time of the month I can be myself.

—*Roseanne Barr*

Most men act so tough and strong on the outside because on the inside, we are scared, weak, and fragile. Men, not women, are the weaker sex.

—*Jerry Rubin*

I'd rather be a woman than a man.
Women can cry, they can wear cute
clothes, and they're first to be rescued
off sinking ships.

—*Gilda Radner*

I have always felt that a woman has the
right to treat the subject of her age with
ambiguity until, perhaps, she passes
into the realm of over ninety. Then it is
better she be candid with herself and
with the world.

—*Helena Rubinstein*

Watch out for men who have mothers.

—*Laura Shapiro*

Men and women, women and men. It
will never work.

—*Erica Jong*

The ideal man has the strength of men
and the compassion of women.

—*The Zohar*

No one will ever win the battle of the sexes; there's too much fraternizing with the enemy.

—*Henry Kissinger*

The great question, which I have not been able to answer, despite my thirty years in research into the feminine soul, is "What does a woman want?"

—*Sigmund Freud*

Like a gold ring in a pig's snout, is a beautiful woman who lacks discretion.

—*Proverbs*

To be successful, a woman has to be much better at her job than a man.

—*Golda Meir*

When women are depressed they either eat or go shopping.
Men invade another country.

—*Elayne Boosler*

Women need a reason to have sex.
Men, they just need a place.

—*Billy Crystal*

While men control the history of
nations and civilizations, women use
family history as their negotiable
instruments.

—*Letty Cottin Pogrebin*

The girl who can't dance says the band
can't play.

Good girls go to heaven, bad girls go
everywhere.

—*Mae West*

Every man I meet wants to protect me.
I can't figure out what from.

—*Mae West*

You know, she speaks eighteen
languages. And she can't say
'No' in any of them.

—*Dorothy Parker*

Beware of the man who wants to protect you; he will protect you from everything but himself.

—*Erica Jong*

To facilitate a union between man and woman is as difficult a task as parting the Red Sea.

—*The Talmud*

Thou shalt not judge a woman by the color of her hair, the wrinkles in her face, or the weight on her body, but rather by the wisdom, inspiration, and love in her soul.

—*Leona Green*

LOVE & MARRIAGE

Love turns one person into two and two into one.

—*Abarbanel*

He who has no wife lives without joy, without blessing, and without good.

—*The Talmud*

Love, by its very nature, is unworldly, and it is for this reason rather than its rarity that it is not only apolitical but anti-political, perhaps the most powerful of all anti-political human forces.

— *Hannah Arendt*

True love comes quietly, without banners or flashing lights. If you hear bells, get your ears checked.

—*Erich Segal*

If your wife is short, bend down and
listen to her.

—*The Talmud*

The magic of first love is our ignorance
that it can never end.

—*Benjamin Disraeli*

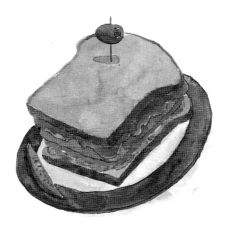

I wanted someone to share my sandwich with. And it had to be marriage and not just living together because I didn't want him to eat and run.

—*Betty Rollin*

A Code of Honor: Never approach a friend's girlfriend or wife with mischief as your goal. There are just too many women in the world to justify that sort of dishonorable behavior. Unless she's really attractive.

—*Bruce Jay Friedman*

I think men who have a pierced ear are better prepared for marriage. They've experienced pain and bought jewelry.

—*Rita Rudner*

Set me as a seal on your heart,
    As a seal on your arm;
For love is strong as death.

—*Song of Songs*

Hatred stirs up strife,
But love covers all wrongs.

—*Proverbs*

Even in Paradise, it's not good to be alone.

The only true love is love at first sight;
second sight dispels it.

—*Israel Zangwill*

Love is not blind—it sees more, not
less. But because it sees more,
it is willing to see less.

—*Rabbi Julie Gordon*

Love is sweet,
but tastes better with bread.

—*Yiddish Proverb*

Love is the answer. But while you're
waiting for the answer, sex brings up
some pretty good questions.

—*Woody Allen*

Marriage is not merely sharing the
fettucini, but sharing the burden of
finding the fettucini restaurant in the
first place.

—*Calvin Trillin*

See, an ugly person who goes after a pretty person gets nothing but trouble. But a pretty person who goes after an ugly person gets at least cab fare.

—*Harvey Fierstein*

Politics doesn't make strange bedfellows, marriage does.

—*Groucho Marx*

Love is not the dying moan
of a distant violin—it's the triumphant
twang of a bedspring.

—*S. J. Perelman*

Eighty percent of married men
cheat in America.
The rest cheat in Europe.

—Jackie Mason

A man died and his wife phoned the
newspaper to place an obituary.
She called the obituary department and
said, "This is what I want to print:
Bernie is dead." The man at the newspaper said, "But for $25 you are
allowed to print six words." The woman
answered, "OK. Then print: Bernie is
dead. Toyota for sale."

Sadie's husband Jake has been slipping in and out of a coma for several months, yet his faithful wife stays by his bedside day and night. One night, Jake comes to and motions for her to come closer. He says, "My Sadie, you have been with me through all the bad times. When I got fired, you were there to support me. When my business failed, you were there. When I got shot, you were by my side. When we lost the house, you gave me support. When my health started failing, you were still by my side. You know what, Sadie?" "What dear?" she asked gently. "I think you're bad luck."

A woman who is loved always
has success.

—*Vicki Baum*

Love is everything that enhances,
widens, and enriches our life.

—*Franz Kafka*

If a woman says, "My husband is distasteful to me, and I cannot have intercourse with him," he is compelled to grant her a divorce, because she is not to be considered a captive woman who must satisfy her husband.

—*Moses Maimonides*

Honor your wives that you may be enriched.

—*The Talmud*

Every man gets the wife he deserves.

—*The Talmud*

Forty days before an embryo is formed, a heavenly voice proclaims: the daughter of so-and-so will be the wife of so-and-so.

—*The Talmud*

If you want to know about a man, you can find out an awful lot by looking at the woman he married.

—*Kirk Douglas*

Because a man is unfaithful to you is no reason to leave him. You should stay with him and make sure the rest of his life is a living hell.

—*Roseanne Barr*

I have never called my wife "wife" but "home."

—*The Talmud*

All love that depends on some material cause, and the material cause passes away, the love vanishes too; but if it does not depend on some material cause, it will never pass away.

—*Ethics of the Fathers*

House and riches are an inheritance from fathers, But a prudent wife is from God.

—*Proverbs*

We are all born for love.
It is the principle of existence,
and its only end.

—*Benjamin Disraeli*

An angry man sleeps alone.

JEWS AND NON-JEWS

There's only one difference between Catholics and Jews. Jews are born with guilt, and Catholics have to go to school to learn it.

—*Elayne Boosler*

WASPs leave and never say good-bye. Jews say good-bye and never leave.

Yossi, a very religious young Jew, left his village in the old country to seek his fortune in America. Years later, after having made good, he decided to return home visit his parents. "Yossele, I barely recognize you," said his mother upon first seeing him. "Mama, my name is John now." "But, my Yossele, why aren't you wearing a beard like a good Jew?" "In America, all men are clean-shaven." "At least you're keeping a kosher home, my child?" "To tell you the truth, Mama, it's nearly impossible to follow the dietary laws." "Tell me, John, are you still circumcised?"

A lot of people say to me,
"Why did you kill Christ?"
"I dunno . . . it was one of those parties,
got out of hand, you know."
"We killed him because he didn't want to
become a doctor, that's why we killed him."

Alright. I'll clear the air once and for
all, and confess. Yes, we did it. I did it,
my family. I found a note in my base-
ment. It said: "We killed him.
Signed, Morty."

—*Lenny Bruce*

The Pope met with the College of Cardinals to discuss a proposal from Shimon Peres, the former leader of Israel. "Your holiness," said one of the Cardinals, "Mr. Peres wants to determine whether Jews or Catholics are superior by challenging you to a golf match." The Pope was greatly disturbed, as he had never held a golf club in his life. "Not to worry," said the Cardinal, "we'll call America and talk to Jack Nicklaus. We'll make him a Cardinal, he can play Shimon Peres. We can't lose!" Everyone agreed it was a good idea. The call was made and, of course, Jack was honored and agreed to play.

The day after the match, Nicklaus reported to the Vatican to inform the

Pope of his success in the match. "I lost, your Holiness," said Nicklaus. "You lost?" exclaimed the surprised Pope. "You lost to Shimon Peres?!!" "No," said Nicklaus, "second to Rabbi Tiger Woods."

I don't think Jews can be born again. A makeover, yes. Bankruptcy is close, but it's not the same thing.

—*Michael Feldman*

Two old Jewish men are walking down the street one day when they happen to walk by a Catholic church. They see a big sign posted in front that says, "Covert to Catholicism and get $1000." One of the Jewish men stops and stares at the sign. His friend turns to him and says, "Murray, what's going on?" "Abe," replies Murray, "I'm thinking of doing it." Abe says, "What are you, crazy?" Murray thinks for a minute and says, "Abe, I'm going to do it." With that, Murray strides purposefully into the church and comes out twenty minutes later with his head bowed. "So," asks Abe, "did you get your thousand dollars?" Murray looks up at him and says, "Is that all you people think about?"

A priest and a rabbi are riding together on the train and they get to talking. After a while, the priest asks the rabbi if he's ever tasted ham. "Yes," he says, "and it was delicious." This emboldens the rabbi so he asks the priest if he's ever made love with a woman. The priest blushes and admits that he did, once, many years ago. "Better than ham, eh?" says the rabbi.

If you ever forget you're a Jew, a Gentile will remind you.

—*Bernard Malamud*

Anti-Semitism is not to be overcome by
getting people to forget us,
but to know us.

—Meyer Levin

I remember my Catholic school days.
Now, that was awful. You know, being a
Jew and all. They wouldn't let me take
Communion. They said, "You killed
him, you can't eat him, too."

—Betsy Salkind

During WWII, a Southern woman calls
an army base to invite five soldiers for
Thanksgiving dinner.
"Just make sure there are no Jews,"
she tells the sergeant.
On Thanksgiving, five black soldiers
show up for dinner. "Your sergeant
has made a terrible mistake,"
the woman says. "Oh no, ma'am," one
soldier says, "Sergeant Goldberg never
makes a mistake."

Jews are like everyone else,
only more so.

JEWISH LOGIC

If one man calls you a donkey, ignore him, if two men call you a donkey, think about it. If three men call you a donkey, buy a saddle.

Trying to catch a thief, a rabbi ran up to a group of men and said "I know which one of you did it." "How do you know?" the men asked. "Because the one who did it— his hat is on fire!" After a few moments, one man reached up and grabbed his hat. "A-HA!" cried the rabbi.

An old Jew and a young Jew are traveling on the train. The young Jew asks: "Excuse me, what time is it?" The old Jew does not answer. "Excuse me, sir, what time is it?" The old Jew keeps silent. "Sir, I'm asking you what time is it. Why don't you answer?" The old Jew says, "Son, the next stop is the last on this route. I don't know you, so you must be a stranger. If I answer you now, I'll have to invite you to my home.

You're handsome, and I have a beautiful daughter. You will both fall in love and you will want to get married. Tell me, why would I need a son-in-law who can't even afford a watch?"

There is an element of truth in every idea
that lasts long enough to be called corny.

—*Irving Berlin*

If you want to make peace, you don't
talk to your friends.
You talk to your enemies.

—*Moshe Dayan*

No matter what side of the argument you are on, you always find people on your side that you wish were on the other.

—*Jascha Heifetz*

If a horse with four legs can sometimes stumble, how much more a man with only one tongue.

—*Shalom Aleichem*

In the middle of rush hour, an immigrant peddler keeps searching for something on each corner of Forty-second Street. A policeman walks over to see what's the matter. "I lost a twenty-dollar bill," says the peddler. "On which corner do you think you lost it?" asks the policeman. " I didn't lose it on Forty-second Street, I lost it on Twenty-third Street, but the light's better here."

Bad habits are easier to abandon today than tomorrow.

Bernie walks into a post office to send a package to his wife. The postmaster says, "This package is too heavy. You'll need another stamp." Bernie replies "And that should make it lighter?"

Anything worth saying is worth repeating a thousand times.

A rabbi is listening to two opposing sides of a Talmudic argument. After hearing the first one, he says, "You're right." Then, after hearing the second one, he says "And you're right." Immediately, the rebbetzin butts in: "But Rabbi, they can't both be right!" To which the rabbi replies, "And you're right, too."

Ask about your neighbors,
then buy the house.

IF WE DON'T LAUGH,
WE MUST WEEP

For every ten Jews beating their breasts, God designated one to be crazy and amuse the breast-beaters. By the time I was five I knew I was that one.

—*Mel Brooks*

Jews can't afford to revel in the tragic because it might overwhelm them.

—*Arthur Miller*

In anything Jewish I ever did, I wasn't standing apart, making fun of the race, and what happened to me on the stage is what could happen to them. They identified with me, and then it was all right to get a laugh, because they were laughing at me as well as themselves.

—*Fanny Brice*

Guilt is the gift that keeps on giving.

—*Anonymous*

A Jew was walking on a street in Berlin when he accidentally brushed against a black-shirted storm trooper. "Swine!" roared the Nazi. "Epstein," said the Jew, bowing.

What used to be called liberal is now called radical, what used to be called radical is now called insane, what used to be called reactionary is now called moderate, and what used to be called insane is now called solid conservative thinking.

—*Tony Kushner*

Berlin, 1934. A Nazi SS officer stops an old Jewish man in the street. "Tell me," he says,"Who was responsible for starting the World War?" The old man replies,"The Jews." The Nazi says"Why the bicycle riders?" The old man says,"Why the Jews?"

Saddam Hussein phoned President Clinton and said, "Bill, I called you because I had this incredible dream last night. I could see all of America, and it was beautiful and on top of every building, there was a beautiful banner." Clinton asked, "What was on the banner?" Saddam responded, "It said Allah is God, God is Allah." Clinton said: "You know, Saddam, I'm really glad you called, because last night I had a dream too. I could see all of Baghdad, and it was even more beautiful than before the war. It had been completely rebuilt, and on every building there was also a beautiful banner." Saddam said, "What was on the banner?" Clinton replied, "I really don't know . . . I don't read Hebrew."

Moscow, 1970s. The phone rings at KGB headquarters. "Hello? Hello, is this KGB?" "Yes. What do you want?" "I'm calling to report my neighbor, Schlomo Berkovitz, as an enemy of the State. He is hiding undeclared diamonds in his firewood." Next day, the KGB goons come over to Berkovitz's house. They search the shed where the firewood is kept, break every piece of wood, find no diamonds, swear at Schlomo and leave. The phone rings at Berkovitz's house. "Hello, Schlomo. Did the KGB come?" "Yes." "Did they chop your firewood?" "Yes, they did." "Okay, now it's your turn to call. I need my vegetable patch plowed."

An old Jew was refused service in a restaurant. "We don't serve Jews here," the waiter said. "Don't let that bother you," replied the old man. "I don't eat Jews!"

Vote for the man who promises least. He'll be the least disappointing.

—*Bernard Baruch*

Tragedy is if I cut my finger. Comedy is if you walk into an open sewer and die.

—*Mel Brooks*

I have become my own version of an optimist. If I can't make it through one door, I'll go through another door—or I'll make a door. Something terrific will come no matter how dark the present.

—*Joan Rivers*

Even when I'm sick and depressed, I love life.

—*Arthur Rubenstein*

1943, Auschwitz. Izzie and Max are being led to the gas chamber when the Izzie pulls down his pants, "moons" the guard and yells, "Drop dead, you Nazi bastard!" Max shakes his head and says, "Shah, Izzie, don't make trouble"

A cheerful heart makes good medicine,
but a crushed spirit dries up the bones.

—*Proverbs*

Tears cleanse the heart, but laughter makes it lighter.

Humor is just another defense against the universe.

—*Mel Brooks*

You just can't get through life without a sense of humor these days. The most awful things can really be funny. You have to be able to laugh or it gets too depressing.

—*Margo Kaufman*

FAMILY

To what lengths should the duty of honoring parents go? Even were they to take a purse of his, full of gold, and cast it in his presence into the sea, he must not shame them, manifest grief in their presence, or display any anger, but accept the divine decree without demur . . . . Although children are commanded to go to the above men- tioned lengths, the father is forbidden to impose too heavy a yoke upon them, to be too exacting with them in matters pertaining to his honor, lest he cause them to stumble. He should forgive them and close his eyes; for a father has the right to forego the honor due him.

—*Moses Maimonides*

Let us hope we will both live to see strange and wonderful things. Perhaps we will die before then. Out children will live to see it then.

—*Clifford Odets*

Big families are important when you have trouble in your life.

—*Neil Simon*

My brother's gay. My parents don't
mind as long as he marries a doctor.

—*Elayne Boosler*

A child's wisdom is also wisdom.

The family is the school of duties . . .
founded on love.

—*Felix Adler*

I'm trying to decide whether or not to have children. My time is running out. I know I want to have children while my parents are still young enough to take care of them.

—*Rita Rudner*

My grandmother was a very tough woman. She buried three husbands. Two of them were just napping.

—*Rita Rudner*

The more people have studied different methods of bringing up children the more they have come to the conclusion that what good mothers and fathers instinctively feel like doing for their babies is the best after all.

—*Benjamin Spock*

Each child brings his own blessing into the world.

—*Yiddish saying*

Ask your child what he wants for dinner
only if he is buying.

—*Fran Lebowitz*

Figure it out. Work a lifetime to pay off
a house. You finally own it and there's
no one to live in it.

—*Arthur Miller*

My mother loved children—she would
have given anything if I had been one.

—*Groucho Marx*

Parenthood remains the greatest single preserve of the amateur.

—Alvin Toffler

Train up a child in the way he should go, And when he is old he will not depart from it.

—Proverbs

When we hear the baby laugh, it is the loveliest thing that can happen to us.

—*Sigmund Freud*

Happiness is having a large, loving,
caring, close-knit family in another city.

—*George Burns*

One of life's greatest mysteries is how the boy who wasn't good enough to marry your daughter can be the father of the smartest grandchild in the world.

My father never lived to see his dream come true of an all-Yiddish-speaking Canada.

—*David Steinberg*

A wise son makes a father glad, but a foolish son is the grief of his mother.

—*Proverbs*

Everyday happiness means getting up in the morning, and you can't wait to finish your breakfast. You can't wait to do your exercises. You can't wait to put on your clothes. You can't wait to get out—and you can't wait to come home, because the soup is hot.

—*George Burns*

Small children, small problems: big children, big problems.

Children love to be alone because alone
is where they know themselves, and
where they dream.

—*Roger Rosenblatt*

A Jewish man with parents alive is a fifteen-year-old boy and will remain a fifteen-year-old boy until they die.

—*Philip Roth*

Why, in this post-feminist era, is a father's bond to his son not viewed as deep as a mother's?

—*Judith Hauptman*

Rich I am not, but the little I have I think it my duty to share with my poor mother and father.

—*Haym Salomon*

I once complained to my father that I didn't seem to be able to do things the same way other people did. Dad's advice? "Margo, don't be a sheep. People hate sheep. They eat sheep."

—*Margo Kaufman*

It is the longing for the father that lives in each of us from his childhood days.

—*Sigmund Freud*

I was the same kind of father as I was a harpist—I played by ear.

—*Harpo Marx*

What the child says outdoors, he has learned indoors.

—*The Talmud*

A man should not say to a child, "I will give you something," and then fail to give it to him, because this will teach the child to lie.

—*The Talmud*

To be rooted is perhaps the most important and least recognized need of the human soul.

—*Simone Weil*

FOOD & DRINK

A Jewish man having dinner in a restaurant calls to his waiter "Waiter, taste this soup!" "What are you talking about,?" says the waiter, "There's nothing wrong with the soup." "Just taste it," the man says. The waiter goes to taste the soup. "How can I taste it? There's no spoon," says the waiter. "A-HA!" says the man.

A salad is not a meal. It is a style.

—*Fran Lebowitz*

A sinner is one who deprives
himself of wine.

—*The Talmud*

Koolaid is goyish. All Drake's Cakes are goyish. Pumpernickel is Jewish, and, as you know, white bread is very goyish. Instant potatoes—goyish. Black cherry soda's very Jewish, Macaroons are *very* Jewish—very Jewish cake. Fruit salad is Jewish. Lime Jell-O is goyish. Lime soda is very goyish. Trailer parks are so goyish that Jews won't go near them.

—*Lenny Bruce*

Why don't Jews drink? It interferes with their suffering.

—*Henny Youngman*

A Jewish man and a Chinese man were talking. The Jewish man commented upon what a wise people the Chinese are. "Yes," replied the Chinese man, "Our culture is over 4,000 years old. But, you Jews are a very wise people, too." The Jewish man replied, "Yes, our culture is over 5,000 years old." The Chinese man was incredulous, "That's impossible," he replied. "Where did your people eat for a thousand years?"

He who has fed a stranger may
have fed an angel.

—The Talmud

Short summary of almost every Jewish
Holiday: "They tried to kill us, we won,
let's eat."

Grub first, then ethics.

—Berthold Brecht

Mrs. Goldberg and Mrs. Weiss are
lunching at a well-known Miami Beach
hotel. "The food here is terrible," says
Mrs. Goldberg. "And such small
portions!" adds Mrs. Weiss.

What I love about cooking is that after a hard day, there is something comforting about the fact that if you melt butter and add flour, then hot stock, it will get thick! It's a sure thing. It's a sure thing in a world where nothing is sure!

—*Nora Ephron*

An egg is superior to the same quantity of any other food.

—*The Talmud*

I had left home (like all Jewish girls) in order to eat pork and take birth control pills. When I first shared an intimate evening with my husband I was swept away by the passion (so dormant inside myself) of a long and tortured existence. The physical cravings I had tried so hard to deny finally and ultimately sated . . . but enough about the pork.

—Roseanne Barr

A piece of rye bread isn't very tasty.
A slice of onion isn't such a treat.
A slab of cream cheese tastes a little pasty, but—
With a little bit of lox, with a little bit of lox,
You've got something very good to eat!

—Allan Sherman

When a poor person eats a chicken, one
of them is sick.

If we didn't have to eat, we'd all be rich.

Q: What did the blind man say after being given a piece of matzoh?

A: Who wrote this crap?

The whole word chicken is funny. Every bit of it, funny. The *ch*, the *i*, the *k*. Put it together and you've got the funniest word in the English language. Chicken. There's nothing funnier than chicken. And when Jews say it, it's even funnier, because they say "tzik'n" and they swallow the n at the end which is wonderful.

—*Mel Brooks*

When you're eating tongue, how do you know when you're finished?

—*Elayne Boosler*

As life's pleasures go, food is second only to sex. Except for salami and eggs. Now that's better than sex, but only if the salami is thickly sliced.

—*Alan King*

Better a crust of bread and enjoy it than a cake that gives you indigestion.

—*Gertrude Berg*

Two Jews, Cohen and Bernstein, sit down in a restaurant and the waiter comes over to take their order. "Sirs, what can I get you?" asks the waiter. "A glass of orange juice," says Cohen. "A glass of orange juice for me too" says Bernstein, "and make sure the glass is clean." The waiter eventually returns with two glasses of orange juice. "So," he says, "which one of you wanted the clean glass?"

Fruit is good. Fruit kept me going for 140 years. Mainly nectarines. I love that fruit. It's half peach, half plum. It's a helluva fruit.

—*Mel Brooks*

Sam is on his death bed, with his family gathered around, saying their farewells.

He smells something wonderful. "Sadie," he says to his wife, "what is that delicious aroma?" "It's my apple strudel," she replies, tears in her eyes. "Oh, my dear wife, I just have to have a piece of your strudel one last time." "You can't. It's for after."

ETHICS AND JUSTICE

Do not judge alone, for there is none who may judge alone save One.

—*Ethics of the Fathers*

Social justice should have nothing to do with personal likes and dislikes.

—*Sam Levenson*

The wicked are called dead even when they are still alive; the righteous are alive even when they are dead.

—*The Talmud*

It is forbidden even to lift a hand against another, and if one does lift a hand against another, he is deemed wicked even if he does not actually strike him.

—*Moses Maimonides*

Who has much learning but no good deeds is like an unbridled horse, that throws off the rider as soon as he mounts.

—*Ethics of the Fathers*

If we don't believe in freedom of expression for people we despise, we don't believe in it at all.

—*Noam Chomsky*

Oral deception is more heinous than monetary fraud because restoration is possible in the latter while no restoration is possible in the former, and the latter concerns one's money while the former affects his person.

—*Moses Maimonides*

The purpose of the laws of the Torah
is . . . to promote compassion,
loving-kindness and peace in the world.

—*Moses Maimonides*

I generally avoid temptation unless I can't resist it.

—*Mae West*

If you're going to do something wrong,
at least enjoy it.

A generation in which human ideals do
not improve must perish.

—*The Koretser Rabbi*

Truth has no special time of its own. Its
hour is now—always.

—*Albert Schweitzer*

Without law, civilization perishes.

—*Talmud*

I'm very critical of the U.S., but get me outside the country and all of a sudden I can't bring myself to say one nasty thing about it.

—*Saul Alinsky*

It is easier to fight for one's principles than to live up to them.

—*Alfred Adler*

The most violent element in society is ignorance.

—*Emma Goldman*

Wherever they burn books they will also, in the end, burn human beings.

—*Heinrich Heine*

You can wash your hands but not your conscience.

Through the wars and massacres of our era people have kept worrying about the ethics of executing a man guilty of murder. It shows how we cling to a theory of civilized behavior while violating it up and down the earth.

—*Ben Hecht*

These are my principles. If you don't like them I have others.

—*Groucho Marx*

The heart is often a lonely voice in the marketplace of living. Men may entertain lofty ideals and behave like the ass that, as the saying goes, "carries gold and eats thistles." The problem of the soul is how to live nobly in an animal environment; how to persuade and train the tongue and the senses to behave in agreement with the insights of the soul.

—*Abraham Joshua Heschel*

You can't chew with someone else's teeth.

Never let your sense of morals get in the way of doing what's right.

—*Isaac Asimov*

If I am not for myself, then who will be for me? And if I am only for myself, then what am I? And if not now, when?

—*Rabbi Hillel*

Be the master of your will and the slave of your conscience.

The more flesh, the more worms; the more possessions, the more anxiety; the more wives, the more witchery; the more maidservants, the more lasciviousness; the more manservants, the more robbery; the more study of the Law, the more life; the more schooling, the more wisdom; the more counsel, the more understanding; the more charity, the more peace.

—*Rabbi Hillel*

A half truth is a whole lie.

Despise not any man, and discard not any thing, for there is not a man who has not his hour and there exists not a thing which has not its place.

—Ethics of the Fathers

There are three crowns: the crown of the Law, the crown of priesthood, and the crown of royalty, but the crown of a good name surpasses them all.

—Ethics of the Fathers

The day is short and the task is great.

—*Ethics of the Fathers*

It is not in our power to explain either the prosperity of the wicked or the tribulations of the righteous.

—*Ethics of the Fathers*

A man is not honest just because he has had no chance to steal.

Judge a man only by his own deeds and
words; the opinions of
others can be false.

—*The Talmud*

If you're not prepared to defend it in
public, don't do it.

—*Alan Dershowitz*

BLESSINGS

We don't need any more commandments,
but more blessings, always!

—*Mei Mei Sanford*

May you be like Sarah, Rebecca,
Rachel, and Leah.

Prayer is greater than sacrifices.

—*The Talmud*

He who recites a blessing
is blessed himself.

—*The Talmud*

If you bless the Lord with joy, He will
bless you with joy and plenty. He who
receives enjoyment in this world without blessing God for it, robs both the
Lord and the congregation of Israel.

—*The Talmud*

May the Lord bless you,
May He watch over you,
May the Lord make
His face shine upon you,
May He be gracious to you.
May the Lord lift up
His face to you and give you peace.

—*Blessing of the Cohanim*

May you have a good year and be written
in the Book of Life.

—*Greeting on Rosh Hashanah*

Next year in Jerusalem.

—*Passover Haggadah*

May you celebrate your birthday in old age.

May health and contentment be your portion to the end of your days.

May God bless and keep the Czar . . . far away from us.

—*Fiddler on the Roof*

May your days glide away free from trouble.

May you live long enough to celebrate
your hundredth birthday.

Wear it in good health!

May God bless and keep you always,
May your wishes all come true,
May you always do for others
And let others do for you.
May you build a ladder to the stars
And climb on every rung,
May you stay forever young.

—*Bob Dylan*

Peace be upon you.

May you live and be well.

May you stay well.

May you live till 100, like a
twenty-year old.

You should live till 120.

May you never know from hunger.

May you never know from sorrow.

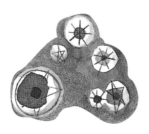

A blessing on your head.

May we meet on happy occasions.

May your strength continue.

He's the right sort of pepper.

Curses and Insults

May you lose all your teeth but one, and may that one have a cavity.

May you put your shoes on backwards, and get a bloody nose when you walk into yourself.

May you have a lot of money, but be the only one in your family with it.

Go bang your head against the wall.

She was a whore in her
mother's stomach.

May your sister go begging with every
door shut against her.

Some people are electrifying—they light
up a room when they leave.

May he grow like an onion . . . with his
head in the ground and his feet
in the air!

May your mother be destined to take
her meals at strange tables.

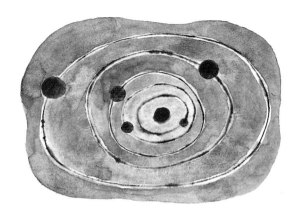

Two things are infinite: the universe
and human stupidity; and I'm not sure
about the universe.

—*Albert Einstein*

He should burn up!

A plague on you—may you get the cholera!

May you go to a different doctor every day
and never know what's wrong with you.

A curse on my enemies!

You should choke on it!

Go drive yourself crazy!

You should explode.

Go take a bath!

He should drop dead!

Drive yourself crazy, not me!

You should get a stomach cramp!

A miserable year you should have.

He opens his mouth and the whole
Bronx could fall in!

Your life should be a disaster!

If I ever speak to you again, may my
tongue fall out of my mouth!

They've buried nicer looking people
than that.

When a bore leaves the room, you feel
as if someone came in.

An elderly Jewish woman is leaving
garment district to go home from
work. Suddenly a man who has been
walking towards her stands in front of
her, blocks her path, opens up his
raincoat and flashes her. Unruffled,
she takes a look and remarks, "You call
that a lining?"

Do me a favor and drop dead.

May onions grow from your navel.

They have an IQ of 160 between them.

You should have a rupture in
your stomach.

You should hang and burn like a
chandelier.

May you have a large business; what people want, you should never have, and what you have to sell, people will never want to buy.

Your store should burn down, and your house with it. Your family should starve. Your wife should scrub floors for Ukrainians. Your daughters should sell themselves on the street. Your sons should marry shicksas. And if you make a dollar, it should go to the doctors.

The nuisance is here already!

He is a low down good-for-nothing!

Go peddle your fish elsewhere!

He eats as if he has just recovered from
a sickness!

If his word were a bridge, it'd be better
not to cross.

From your mouth to God's ears.

He's a big nothing.

May a buffalo in heat find you in his time of need.

His ignorance is encyclopedic.

—*Abba Eban*

He should go to hell!

It shouldn't happen to a dog.

You should swell up like a mountain.

Cynicism is what passes for insight
among the mediocre.

—*Joe Klein*

CHARITY & COMMUNITY

Do not separate yourself from the community and do not be sure of yourself until the day of your death.

—*Rabbi Hillel*

Whosoever gives charity to a poor man ill-manneredly and with downcast looks has lost all the merit of his action even though he should give him a thousand gold pieces.

—*Moses Maimonides*

The world is not comprehensible, but it is embraceable: through the embracing of one of its beings.

—*Martin Buber*

People's good deeds are used by the Eternal as seeds for planting trees in the Garden of Eden: thus, each of us creates our own Paradise.

—*The Mezeritzer Rebbe*

We gave to the poor regularly. It made us feel rich.

—*Sam Levenson*

The true measure of a man is how he treats someone who can do him absolutely no good.

—*Ann Landers*

I feel that the greatest reward for doing
is the opportunity to do more.

—*Jonas Salk*

To give aid to every poor man is far
beyond the reach and power of every
man. Care of the poor is incumbent on
society as a whole.

—*Baruch Spinoza*

Through charity and kindness a man
attains to godliness.

—*Rabbi Nachman of Bretslav*

The greatest charity is to enable the
poor to earn a living.

—*The Talmud*

Say little and do much.

—*The Talmud*

Nobody is ever impoverished through the giving of charity.

—*Moses Maimonides*

The best exercise for strengthening the heart is to reach down and lift others up.

—*Morris Mandel*

Even a poor man who lives off charity should perform acts of charity.

—*The Talmud*

If charity cost nothing, the world would be full of philanthropists.

I know that there are people who do not love their fellow man, and I hate people like that!

—*Tom Lehrer*

In any free society where terrible wrongs exist, some are guilty—all are responsible.

—*Abraham Joshua Heschel*

He who executes charity and justice is
regarded as though he had filled the
entire world with kindness.

—*The Talmud*

Who can protest and does not is an
accomplice in the act.

—*The Talmud*

The commandment to be charitable is
in its weight as much as all the rest of
the commandments in total.

—*The Talmud*

He who gives a coin to a poor man obtains six blessings, but he who addresses him with words of comfort obtains eleven blessings.

—*The Talmud*

Cast your bread upon the waters; for after many days you will find it.

—*Solomon*

The whole world is one town.

One who gives to the poor has no lack; but one who closes his eyes will have many curses.

—*Proverbs*

To smile at your neighbor is more
important than to offer him a drink.

—*The Talmud*

BEING JEWISH

If you live in New York or any other big city, you are Jewish. It doesn't matter even if you're Catholic, if you live in New York, you're Jewish.

—Lenny Bruce

On Judgment Day, a man will have to
give account for every good thing that
his eye saw and he did not enjoy.

—*The Talmud*

What is hateful to yourself, do not do to
your neighbor. That is the whole of the
Torah. The rest is commentary. Now go
and study.

—*Rabbi Hillel*

Only a Jew can ask a question and
answer it in the same sentence.

There was a time when I couldn't find roots because I was ashamed to look at where they were. When you are running around Madison Avenue, when you are lunching at Louis & Armand's or Michael's Pub, you carefully avoid mentioning your Grandfather, the Ladies' Coat Presser, and your Grandmother, the Poker Player . . . . When you're at a cocktail party in the Waldorf Towers and they pass you the goose-lover pate, you very carefully neglect to point out that Lindy's chopped chicken liver tastes a lot better to you. You cover up the old roots because something in your own upbringing has convinced you that they are weeds . . . .

—*Allan Sherman*

Nobody is stronger, nobody is weaker than someone who came back. There is nothing you can do to such a person because whatever you could do is less than what has already been done to him. We have already paid the price.

—*Elie Wiesel*

You can get used to anything if you have to, even to feeling perpetually guilty.

—*Golda Meir*

Where two Jews, three opinions.

Since we long ago resolved never to be servants to the Romans, nor to any other than to God Himself, Who alone is the true and just Lord of mankind, the time is now come that obliges us to make that resolution true in practice . . . . We were the very first that revolted, and we are the last to fight against them; and I cannot but esteem it as a favor that God has granted us, that it is still in our power to die bravely, and in a state of freedom.

—*Elazar ben Yair*

Cast us into iron chains, tear us apart like bloody beasts—you can only kill our bodies, you will never destroy our spirit.

—*David Edelstadt*

While legends or their details may not be fully accurate or even true, they serve to characterize both the people and the times.

—*Rabbi Berel Wein*

We do not have to account to anybody, we are not to sit for anybody's examination and nobody is old enough to call on us to answer. We came before them and will leave after them. We are what we are, we are good for ourselves, we will not change and we do not want to.

—*Zev Jabotinsky*

Our way is not soft grass, it's a mountain path with lots of rocks. But it goes upward, forward, toward the sun.

—*Ruth Westheimer*

(The past is) our cradle, not our prison; there is danger as well as appeal in its glamour. The past is for inspiration, not imitation, for continuation, not repetition.

—*Israel Zangwill*

I see Judaism as a huge tree that has been growing for five thousand years If I don't pass the religion on, one of its branches will dead-end with me.

—*Susan Seidelman*

A man asks his fellow passenger on a train, "Are you Jewish?" "No, I'm not," the man replies. A few stops later, the first man asks again, "Are you sure you're not Jewish?" The other replies in the negative again. Finally, as they near the end of the line, the first man can't bear it anymore. "You must be Jewish!" he exclaims. "All right, all right, I'm Jewish, it's true," the other cries. The first man replies, "Funny, you don't look Jewish!"

A Jew and a hunchback are walking past a synagogue. The Jew says "I used to be a Jew." The hunchback then says, "I used to be a hunchback."

We must always take sides. Neutrality
helps the oppressor, never the victim.
Silence encourages the tormentor,
never the tormented.

—*Elie Wiesel*

Jews were not put here just to fight
Anti-Semitism.

—*Rabbi Joseph P. Soloveitchik*

Sure we were chosen, but for what? On
balance, it's been an honor we could
have lived without.

—*Michael Feldman*

The pursuit of knowledge for its own sake, an almost fanatical love of justice, and a desire for personal independence—these are features of the Jewish tradition which make me thank my stars that I belong to it.

—*Albert Einstein*

In spite of everything, I still believe people are really good at heart.

—*Anne Frank*

A people that has learned to live without a country is unconquerable.

—*Israel Zangwill*

The gravest sin is for a Jew to forget—or not to know—what he represents.

—*Abraham Joshua Heschel*

I have come to believe that after the Holocaust there is no place for ambivalent Jewishness.

—*Erica Jong*

Not the power to remember, but its very opposite, the power to forget, is a necessary condition for our existence.

—*Sholem Asch*

In everyone's life, at some time, our inner fire goes out. It is then burst into flame by an encounter with another human being. We should all be thankful for those people who rekindle the inner spirit.

—*Albert Schweitzer*

Being Jewish is sort of what it is being a New Yorker to me. Jewish culture, history, Jewish neuroses, Jewish food, whatever—it's very rich stuff that gives texture to your life.

—*Neil Postman*

Jazz is Irving Berlin, Al Jolson, George Gershwin, Sophie Tucker. These are Jews with roots in the synagogue . . . . You find the soul of a people in the songs they sing.

—*Samson Raphaelson*

Advice & Observations

When in doubt, act like Myrna Loy.

—*Cynthia Heimel*

The more valuable the thing, the more effort it demands.

—*Saadia Gaon*

To pull a man out of the mud, a friend must set foot in that mud.

—*Rabbi Nachman of Bretslav*

When you have to stand on your head to
make someone happy,
all you'll get is a headache.

It is said that stories can help put you to
sleep. I say stories can help
wake you up!

—*Rabbi Nachman of Bretslav*

The sun will set without your help.

Life is ten percent what you make it and ninety percent how you take it.

—*Irving Berlin*

Shrouds have no pockets.

There are worse crimes than burning books. One of them is not reading them.

—*Joseph Brodsky*

When we can't dream any longer,
we die.

—*Emma Goldman*

Just because nobody complains doesn't
mean all parachutes are perfect.

—*Benny Hill*

Advice is what we ask for when we really
know the answer but wish we didn't.

—*Erica Jong*

Be true to your teeth and they won't be
false to you.

—*Soupy Sales*

The world is a narrow bridge. The key
to crossing it is not to be afraid.

—*Rabbi Nachman of Bretslav*

Never trust the man who tells you all his
troubles but keeps from you all his joys.

Miracles sometime occur, but one has
to work terribly hard for them.

—*Chaim Weizmann*

A man should go on living—if only to
satisfy his curiosity.

It is inevitable that some defeat will enter
even the most victorious life.
The human spirit is never finished when it is
defeated . . . is finished when it surrenders.

—*Ben Stein*

Experience is a good school, but the fees are high.

—*Heinrich Heine*

When choosing between two evils, I always like to try the one I've never tried before.

—*Mae West*

Schizophrenia is better than eating alone.

—*Oscar Levant*

Some problems never get solved. They just get older.

—*Chaim Weizmann*

Few are those who see their own faults.

—*The Talmud*

Give every man the benefit of the doubt.
—*The Talmud*

Beauty is a quality, not a form; a content, not an arrangement.

—*Irving Howe*

The meaning of life is that it stops.

—*Franz Kafka*

I make it my business not to make people angry, not to laugh at them, but to seek to understand them.

—*Baruch Spinoza*

That's what life is: a collection of rare and unusual moments , like an array of gems set out before you.

—*Sandra Bernhard*

All excellent things are as difficult as they are rare.

—*Baruch Spinoza*

Even the greatest swimmer can drown.

You can't ride two horses with one behind.

Being entirely honest with oneself is a
good exercise.

—*Sigmund Freud*

Most of the things worth doing in the
world have been declared impossible
before they were done.

—*Louis Brandeis*

Life is something to do when you can't get to sleep.

—*Fran Lebowitz*

Give me the strength to commit my fair share of sins. Then give me the strength to make amends for all of these wrongdoings and to regret them wholeheartedly.

—*Rabbi Aryeh Leib ben Sarah*

If you want people to like you, agree with them.

When pride comes, then comes shame,
But with humility comes wisdom.

—Proverbs

Drink water out of your own cistern,
running water out of your own well.

A fool shows his annoyance the same
day, But one who overlooks an
insult is prudent.

—Proverbs

Even a fool, when he keeps silent, is counted wise.

—*Proverbs*

Better is a dry morsel with quietness, than a house full of feasting with strife.

—*Proverbs*

That which you see and hear, you cannot help; but that which you say depends on you alone.

—*Zohar*

Words are powerful enough to lead to love, but can lead to hatred and terrible pain as well. We must be extremely careful how we use them.

—*Rabbi Joseph Telushkin*

Who finds a faithful friend finds a treasure.

—*Ben Sira*

It is not good to eat much honey; nor is it honorable to seek ones own honor.

—*Proverbs*

I can retract what I did not say, but I cannot retract what I already have said.

—*Solomon Ibn Gabirol*

In the service of life, sacrifice becomes grace.

—*Albert Einstein*

The real voyage of discovery consists not in seeking new lands, but in seeing with new eyes.

—*Marcel Proust*

Better a neighbor who is near, than a brother who is far.

—*Proverbs*

When brains are needed, muscles won't help.

Don't send a cat to deliver cream.

The man who makes arrows is often slain by one of them.

—*The Talmud*

The test of good manners is to be patient with bad ones.

—*Solomon Ibn Gabirol*

If I try to be like him, who will be like me?

—*Yiddish Proverb*

The chief danger in life is that you may take too many precautions.

—*Alfred Adler*

There are three kinds of lies: Lies, Damn Lies, and Statistics.

—*Benjamin Disraeli*

Guilt is a rope that wears thin.

—*Ayn Rand*

Not everything that can be counted counts, and not everything that counts can be counted.

—*Albert Einstein*

Pick battles big enough to matter, but small enough to win.

—*Jonathan Kozol*

Life is a great big canvas; throw all the paint you can at it.

—*Danny Kaye*

Those who do not know how to weep
with their whole heart don't know how
to laugh either.

—*Golda Meir*

If a person feels he can't communicate,
the least he can do is shut up about it.

—*Tom Lehrer*

Happiness isn't something you experience; it's something you remember.

—*Oscar Levant*

Outside of a dog, a book is a man's best friend. And inside of a dog, it's too dark to read.

—*Groucho Marx*

When the only tool you have is a hammer, every problem begins to resemble a nail.

—*Abraham Maslow*

Don't try to be different. Just be good. To be good is different enough.

—*Arthur Freed*

Life is like a sewer—what you get out of it depends on what you put into it.

—*Tom Lehrer*

Sloppy thinking gets worse over time.

—*Jenny Holzer*

The trouble with talking too fast is you may say something you haven't thought of yet.

—*Ann Landers*

Everyone is kneaded out of the same dough but not baked in the same oven.

—*Yiddish Proverb*

Nobody ever died of laughter.

—*Max Beerbohm*

Never be bullied into silence. Never allow yourself to be made a victim. Accept no one's definition of your life; define yourself.

—*Harvey Fierstein*

There are surely worse things than being wrong, and being dull and pedantic are surely among them.

—*Mark Kac*

Life is made up of small pleasures. Happiness is made up of those tiny successes—the big ones come too infrequently. If you don't have all of those zillions of tiny successes, the big ones don't mean anything.

—*Norman Lear*

What soap is for the body,
tears are for the soul.

—*Jewish proverb*

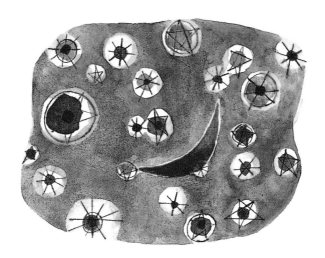

A man can only do what he can do. But
if he does that each day he can sleep at
night and do it again the next day.

—*Albert Schweitzer*

The absence of alternatives clears the mind marvelously.

—*Henry Kissinger*

My advice is to slow down, relax, and smell the lox and onions.

—*Mel Brooks*

The cure for boredom is curiosity. There is no cure for curiosity.

—*Dorothy Parker*

Well-timed silence is the most commanding expression.

—*Mark Helprin*

Pictures are for entertainment, messages should be delivered by Western Union.

—*Samuel Goldwyn*

In a world we find terrifying, we ratify that which doesn't threaten us.

—*David Mamet*

Many years ago a very wise man named Bernard Baruch took me aside and put his arm around my shoulder. "Harpo, my boy," he said, "I'm going to give you three pieces of advice, three things you should always remember." My heart jumped and I glowed with expectation. I was going to hear the magic password to a rich, full life from the master himself. "Yes, sir?" I said. And he told me the three things. I regret that I've forgotten what they were.

—*Harpo Marx*

Just because you're paranoid doesn't mean they're not out to get you.

—*Abbie Hoffman*

One of the rewards of a good friendship is an almost total ignorance of your friend's flaws.

—*Ben Hecht*

A goat may have a beard, but he's still a goat.

Just because I said that's what I want
doesn't mean that I'm ready for it.

—*Harvey Fierstein*

The surest defense against Evil is
extreme individualism, originality of
thinking, whimsicality, even—if you
will—eccentricity. That is, something
that can't be feigned, faked, imitated;
something even a seasoned impostor
couldn't be happy with.

—*Joseph Brodsky*

The optimist thinks this is the best of all possible worlds. The pessimist fears it is true.

—*J. Robert Oppenheimer*

Happiness isn't something you experience; it's something you remember.

—*Oscar Levant*

Learning from experience is a faculty almost never practiced.

—*Barbara Tuchman*

Good sense about trivialities is better than nonsense about things that matter.

—*Max Beerbohm*

Rabbi Zusya said that on the Day of Judgment, God would ask him, not why he had not been Moses, but why he had not been Zusya.

—*Walter Kaufmann*

All's well that ends well.

—*The Talmud*

Slow down and enjoy life. It's not only the scenery you miss by going too fast— you also miss the sense of where you are going and why.

—*Eddie Cantor*

One who looks for a friend without faults will have none.

What you don't see with your eyes, don't witness with your mouth.

An honest answer is the sign of true friendship.

—*Proverbs*

Ducking for apples—change one letter and it's the story of my life.

—*Dorothy Parker*

I have had dreams and I have had nightmares, but I have conquered my nightmares because of my dreams.

—*Dr. Jonas Salk*

The intelligent man who is proud of his intelligence is like the condemned man who is proud of his large cell.

—*Simone Weil*

Truth is the safest lie.

You want to hear what my truth is?
Everything hurts. Whatever it is you get
good in life, you also lose something.

—*Neil Simon*

The way you treat yourself sets the stan-
dard for others.

—*Sonya Friedman*

Sit down again. Don't be afraid of
softness, of sorrow.

—*Clifford Odets*

An ounce of attention is worth a pound
of cure.

—*Groucho Marx*

The laziest man is he who does not seek to acquire friends; still lazier is the one who loses friends because he makes no effort to keep them.

The worst informer is the face.

Let us be grateful to people who make us happy; they are the charming gardeners who make our souls blossom.

—*Marcel Proust*

I was always looking outside myself for strength and confidence but it comes from within. It is there all the time.

—*Anna Freud*

At the baths, all are equal.

Although one should not believe in superstitions, it is better to be careful.

The only way to escape the personal corruption of praise is to go on working.

—*Albert Einstein*

If one is destined to drown, one will drown in a spoonful of water.

If you lie down with dogs, you get up with fleas.

It takes far less courage to kill yourself
than it takes to make yourself wake up
one more time.

—*Judith Rossner*

Houseguests and fish spoil on the third day.

I never think of the future. It comes
soon enough.

—*Albert Einstein*

I don't believe in accidents.
There are only encounters in history.
There are no accidents.

—Elie Wiesel

The rose grows among thorns.

—The Talmud

A name made great is a name destroyed.

—Rabbi Hillel

Creative minds always have been known
to survive any kind of bad training.

—Anna Freud

Life is about not knowing, having to
change, taking the moment and making
the best of it, without knowing what's
going to happen next.
Delicious ambiguity.

—Gilda Radner

Life beats down and crushes the soul
and art reminds you that you have one.

—*Stella Adler*

Beauty comes in all sizes,
not just size five.

—*Roseanne Barr*

Happy is harder than money. Anyone
who thinks money will make them
happy, doesn't have money.

—*David Geffen*

If you have class, you've got it made. If you don't have class, no matter what else you have, it won't make up for it.

—*Ann Landers*

Neurosis seems to be a human privilege.

—*Sigmund Freud*

Don't go into any water where your feet can't touch the bottom.

—*Mel Brooks*

If you keep saying things are going to be bad, you have a chance of being a prophet.

—*Isaac Bashevis Singer*

A loud voice cannot compete with a clear voice, even if it's a whisper.

—*Barry Neil Kaufman*

Blackman, Philip, F.C.S., trans. *Ethics of the Fathers*. New York: Judaica Press, Ltd., 1985.

Bukiet, Melvin Jules, ed. *Neurotica: Jewish Writers on Sex*. New York: W.W. Norton, 1999.

Rosten, Leo. *The Joys of Yiddish*. New York: Pocket, 1991.

Falk, Marcia. *The Book of Blessings: New Jewish Prayers for Daily Life, The Sabbath, And The New Moon Festival*. Boston: Beacon Press, 1999.

Ausubel, Nathan, ed. *A Treasury of Jewish Folklore: Stories, Traditions, Legends, Humor, Wisdom and Folk Songs of the Jewish People*. Revised Edition. New York: Crown Publishers, 1989.

Spalding, Henry D., ed. *Encyclopedia of Jewish Humor: From Biblical Times to the Modern Age*. New York: Jonathan David Publishers, 1969